HAL LEONARD PIANO LIBRARY

J.S. BACH
FIRST LESSONS IN BACH
28 Pieces

Edited and Recorded by Christos Tsitsaros

T0071531

To access companion recorded performances online, visit:
www.halleonard.com/mylibrary

Enter Code
3137-2373-3092-9159

On the cover:
Leipzig Before 1800
artist unknown

© Leonard de Selva, photographer/CORBIS

ISBN 978-1-4234-4672-9

G. SCHIRMER, Inc.

DISTRIBUTED BY

HAL•LEONARD®
CORPORATION

7777 W. BLUEMOUND RD. P.O. BOX 13819 MILWAUKEE, WI 53213

www.musicsalesclassical.com
www.halleonard.com

CONTENTS

The price of this publication includes access to companion recorded performances online, for download or streaming, using the unique code found on the title page. Visit **www.halleonard.com/mylibrary** and enter the access code.

PERFORMANCE NOTES

This edition of *First Lessons in Bach* features a blend of easy to moderately difficult dances drawn from the *Notebook for Anna Magdalena Bach* and the following works by Johann Sebastian Bach: French Suites No. 2 in C minor (BWV 813), No. 5 in G Major (BWV 816), and No. 6 in E Major (BWV 817); English Suites No. 3 in G minor (BWV 808), No. 5 in E minor (BWV 810), and No. 6 in D Major (BWV 811); the Suite in F Minor (BWV 823); Overtures in F Major (BWV 820) and G minor (BWV 822); and Lute Suite No. 1 in E minor (BWV 996). The lighthearted, melodious, and highly colorful character of these brilliant miniatures will delight and musically nourish piano students of all ages; indeed this collection forms an ideal link between the earliest Bach pieces and the more intricate Two-Part Inventions.

Style and Interpretation

A study of the origin and character of each dance is indispensable in clarifying some interpretive issues and problems inherent in the music. Like the *Notebook for Anna Magdalena Bach*, many of Bach's suites incorporate dances of French origin which were added to the standard allemande and courante during the seventeenth century by the French court ballet. These include the following:

- Minuet—in a moderate 3/4

- Sarabande—in a slow 3/4, of Spanish origin

- Gavotte—in a rather moderate 4/4 with an upbeat of two quarter notes, phrases start and end in the middle of a measure

- Bourrée—in 2/2 with a quarter-note upbeat, quicker than the Gavotte

- Polonaise—in 3/4, features angular dotted rhythm, of Polish origin, also favored by the French and German courts

Repeats of each section of a dance were customary during Bach's time and were often played in an improvised ornamented version.

Tempo

The type of dance and the relationship between its time signature and rhythmic values constitute the primary considerations for the choice of tempo. The beat in a piece that abounds in short note values (such as a quarter note) tends to be slower than in a piece of the same time signature but containing longer note values and more ornamentation. In his famous treatise *Essay on the True Art of Playing Keyboard Instruments*, Carl Philipp Emanuel Bach advises thinking of the shortest note values when adopting a tempo, making sure that they are given enough time to be articulated distinctly.

It is also important to bear in mind that the nature of the dances excludes the use of ritardando before every double bar. The pulse should remain unchanged throughout all the section endings, with occasional tapering of the tempo only in the final measures.

Articulation

The near total absence of articulation in Bach's music invites the performer to choose between a variety of touches in order to render the "true content and affect of a composition." Among the different types of articulations C.P.E. Bach mentions in his treatise, three are particularly important for performing Bach's music on the modern piano:

- legato—notes are played smoothly with no separation between successive notes

- staccato—notes are shortened in duration at various degrees, depending on the tempo and dynamic

- portato—a slight separation of each note (also known as non-legato)

According to C.P.E Bach, legato playing is most appropriate in "stepwise passages and in the slower moderate tempos" while detached notes are better suited for the allegros. All appoggiaturas in any tempo should be played legato; leaps on the other hand (other than arpeggio passages) suggest a detached articulation. In general, I find that a sensible balance between all three types of articulation is most appropriate for conveying the lively dance character of these pieces. In his book *Keyboard Interpretation from the 14th to the 19th Century*, Howard Ferguson cautions "an excess of legato in performance produces opaque stodginess, and too much staccato makes for a restless lack of continuity."

The articulation markings included in this edition reflect my own preference, and as such they are by no means definitive.

Dynamics and Phrasing

The use of dynamics, although largely left to the performer's taste, is an indispensable element (along with the articulation and the tempo) upon which the essence of a convincing performance depends. The harpsichord's inability to produce graded (inflected) dynamics does not, in my opinion, form a convincing argument against the use of such dynamics when transferring this music to the modern piano.

C.P.E. Bach stated that the highest duty of a performer was to "make the ear conscious of the true affect of a composition." In order to achieve this, he advised performers to listen frequently to soloists and ensembles, clearly pointing to the need to imitate other instruments' expressiveness and ability to vary the range, and to sensitively shape the sound. He also stressed the importance of listening to vocalists and to singing the phrase in order to understand the correct manner of performing melodies.

It is very unlikely that Bach would have abstained from making ample use of all the sound resources of the modern piano, as he used the individual sound properties of the harpsichord and clavichord to enliven melodic contours and illuminate counterpoint in his music. (It must be mentioned that the clavichord, although limited in volume, was perfectly capable of producing inflected dynamics.) Moreover, the texture of the music was written in such a way as to produce certain dynamic effects on the harpsichord: denser textures and chords would naturally sound louder than sections of thinner texture. Unlike the keyboard player of Bach's time, the modern pianist needs to recognize these cues in the music itself, as in the following example.

Scherzo from Partita No. 3 in A minor, BWV 827, mm. 1–5

Some of the considerations that can lead the performer to the choice of appropriate and tasteful dynamics include the following:

- *The shape of the melody.* Ascending and descending melodic patterns can come to life by a gradual and subtle rise and fall of the volume.

- *The use of tension–resolution.* All dissonances such as appoggiaturas, suspensions, and accented non-harmonic tones need to be lightly stressed, followed by a weakening of the sound in the resolution.

- *The phrase structure.* Different motives and sub-phrases can be characterized by dynamic fluctuations. (This is particularly helpful in sequences.)

- *The texture.* Chords or sections containing chords or more voices often suggest a fuller sound, while a thinner texture often suggests a softer sound.

- *The form and underlying harmonic structure.* The binary dance form, with its characteristic key plan, provides opportunities for dynamic gradation and contrast. Similarly, all cadences and phrases with denser, chromatic chords or unexpected harmonic shifts can be highlighted through the use of subtle dynamic changes in ways that render them more meaningful and proportionate to their surrounding chords.

One of the challenges inherent in these pieces is the understanding of the harmonic implications that are not always immediately discernible due to the predominantly two-voice texture. Evidently, there is no hard and fast rule as to the dynamic shape of a phrase, as often the fall and rise of the volume does not correspond to the beginning, middle, or end of a phrase. Likewise, not all phrase endings need to be tapered, nor the melodic peak of a phrase coincide with its loudest point.

Pedal

The use of pedal in Baroque music is an area of dispute between teachers and performers. Used judiciously, touches of pedal can help highlight certain expressive points, facilitate connections, and add depth and prolongation to selected notes and chords. It can also enhance the sound quality in specific ranges of the piano. When applying pedal in Bach's music, extreme care needs to be exercised not to cloud the linear texture or obscure the harmonic transparency. Simultaneous attention to all these considerations requires a high degree of coordination and dexterity, and therefore may be overwhelming for the less advanced player. In such case, the use of pedal is best postponed. Fortunately, all pieces in this volume may be performed equally well either with or without pedal.

Fingering

According to C.P.E Bach "the correct employment of the fingers is inseparably related to the whole art of performance" and that "facility itself hinges on it." The fingerings of the present edition are equally based on the technical and musical aspects of the piece. I find that fingerings that promote a physical sense of connection based on intervallic relations are most suitable for pieces of a lyrical character or pieces that contain more counterpoint. Faster movements with scale passages, arpeggiated figures, and frequent displacements necessitate fingerings that promote ease and smoothness in position changes, as well as strength and clarity of articulation.

Other aspects besides tempo that led me to the choice of fingering include phrasing, articulation, and ornamentation. Upon experimentation, I strongly believe that alternate fingerings feel and often sound differently. Students, as well as more advanced players, are encouraged to experiment with their own fingering solutions that are suited to their unique physical predisposition, level of advancement, and musical concept.

Ornamentation

The realization of ornaments in the present edition is based on the "Explanation of divers signs, showing how to play certain ornaments properly" and the ensuing "applicatio" with which begins J.S. Bach's *The Little Notebook for Wilhelm Friedemann Bach*. C.P.E. Bach's chapter on ornamentation in his *Essay on the True Art of Playing Keyboard Instruments* offers a more detailed explanation of the various ornaments, their proper use and function, as well as possible variants. Following is a brief description of the ornaments found in this volume.

The Trill 〰 〰 *tr*

C.P.E. Bach mentions that "Trills enliven melodies and therefore are indispensable." The trill invariably begins on the tone above the principal note.

The Longer Trill With or Without Suffix

C.P.E. Bach mentions that "The suffix is omitted from successive trills and from trills followed by one or more short notes which are capable of replacing [the suffix notes]."

March in G Major, BWV Appendix 124, mm. 7–9

In some cases the suffix is written out in the music, leaving no doubt about its use.

Gavotte II from English Suite No. 6 in D minor, BWV 811, mm. 1–2

Half or Short Trill (Halb- or Prall-Triller)

This ornament, mentioned by C.P.E. Bach in the chapter titled "Embellishments" in his *Essay*, occurs on descending stepwise three-note legato patterns. According to Bach, "It represents in miniature an enclosed, unsuffixed trill, introduced by either an appoggiatura or a principal note."

As with articulation, it is necessary to be somewhat flexible with ornamentation when teaching less experienced students. C.P.E. Bach was quite sensitive to the technical limitations of a novice player, stating "It is possible, when necessary, to omit any…ornament, even…trills, and arrange matters so that easier ornaments may be substituted for them." For example, the half or short trill can become a useful alternative to the usual execution of trills in stepwise descending passages, such as those in the following excerpts:

Minuet in G Major, BWV Appendix 114, mm.30–32

Polonaise in G Major, BWV Appendix 130, mm. 20–22

In the recording accompanying this edition, I have chosen to play the simplified version in all places where I have suggested this alternative version.

The Mordent

C.P.E. Bach describes the mordent as "…an essential ornament which connects notes, fills them out, and makes them brilliant." In the dances selected here from the *Notebook for Anna Magdalena Bach*, we encounter only the short mordent.

The Appoggiatura

C.P.E. Bach mentions that "Appoggiaturas are among the most essential embellishments. They enhance the harmony as well as the melody [and they] modify chords which would be too simple without them."

Regarding the duration of appoggiaturas, Bach explains, "…they take from a following tone of duple length one-half of its value, and [usually] two-thirds from one of triple length."

March in G Major, BWV Appendix 124, mm. 12–13

Minuet in G Major, BWV Appendix 114, mm. 7–8

Very importantly, C.P.E. Bach mentions that with regard to their execution, "…appoggiaturas are louder than the following tone…," an important expressive detail often overlooked by less experienced players.

The Schleifer (Slide)

Used rather rarely, the slide helps to fill in a leap and consists of two notes that are played before the principal one.

Minuet in D minor, BWV Appendix 132, mm. 5–6

The Turn

Used rather sparingly in the music of Bach, the turn is, according to C.P.E. Bach, "…an easy embellishment which makes melodies both attractive and brilliant," which "…is employed in slow as well as fast movements, and over slurred as well as detached notes." The tempo determines the value of the surrounding notes.

The harmonic context may require the use of accidentals over the symbol.

While adding ornaments in selected places in repeats may add musical interest and excitement, it is equally acceptable to omit certain ornaments that are indicated in the original manuscript or early sources. The significantly heavier action of the modern piano often makes the realization of consecutive ornaments highly problematic, particularly for the younger student. However, this mechanical drawback of the piano is balanced by its more sustained sound quality compared to that of its predecessors, the harpsichord and the clavichord.

On the companion recordings I have adopted both approaches, depending on the tempo and character of the piece, as well as the idiomatic characteristics of the modern instrument.

The Individual Pieces

Minuet in G Major, BWV Appendix 114

This minuet is similar in character to the Minuet in G Major, BWV Appendix 116. The first four measures can be grouped effectively into a single large phrase with a sweeping dynamic curve that leads to the high G in m. 4. This is the only minuet in the series in which the B section begins on the tonic chord.

Minuet in G minor, BWV Appendix 115

The quietly sad and tender character of this minuet, with its descending, stepwise melodic gestures, requires a delicate touch and skillful phrasing to shape the melodic contour. In m. 31, I opted for a simpler, three-note ornament despite the fact that a four-note trill arguably would be stylistically more correct.

Minuet in G Major, BWV Appendix 116

The repetition of the two-measure motive in the beginning of the piece suggests the use of terraced dynamics. At the same time, the octave leap in mm. 2 and 4 imply an agile dancing gesture that is best achieved using a light staccato touch. The B section provides wonderful opportunities for dynamic shading with its shifts to different registers and its inventive harmonic scheme.

Polonaise in G minor, BWV Appendix 119

Majestic in character, this polonaise calls for experimentation with a variety of dynamics, articulations, and tempos. A portato touch on quarter notes will emphasize the rhythmic element, whereas a mixture of staccato and legato articulations for eighth and sixteenth notes will lighten the serious character of the piece somewhat. Noteworthy are the wedge staccato marks (in the manuscript) on the quarter notes in mm. 11 and 13, denoting a heavily accented, sharp attack.

March in D Major, BWV Appendix 122

The charm of this march lies in the rhythmic vitality that results from the metric accent in the left hand and that of the syncopation in the right hand. Crisp staccato eighth notes in both hands in mm. 8 and 21 will evoke a trumpet sound accompanied by a military drum. Because of the quick tempo and the intricate coordination between the two hands, I would favor using the same finger on the left-hand repeated notes in those measures.

Minuets 1, 2, and 3 from Overture in G minor, BWV 822

As the *da capo* signs indicate, all three minuets are intended as a series in the order 1–2–1–3–1. This results in a short *rondeau* form, typical of certain French Baroque suite movements. Another title for the set could have indeed been "*menuet en rondeau.*" If played as a series, the tempo should remain constant in all three minuets with no additional pause in-between.

The second minuet of this series forms a mirror image of the first in that the thematic material of the right and left hands is inversed—passed from hand to hand. Applying a variety of articulations and a clear dynamic differentiation will help define the two voices and bring forth the witty interplay between them.

The final minuet contains elements of the first two, but its broader range and major key give it a more luminous character.

March in G Major, BWV Appendix 124

Although not explicitly indicated from the start, two voices can be traced in the right-hand part in the opening measures. In keeping with the voicing in mm. 2–3, one could envision an upward stem on the first eighth note in the opening measure. If this march were orchestrated, the repeated eighth-note Gs in the lower voice could be assigned to a percussive instrument, perhaps a tambourin, and the upper voice to a melodic one such as a flute or violin. Two elements also appear in the left-hand part. Rhythmic repeated eighth notes in mm. 1–2 imitate the right-hand part and expand in mm. 10–11 and 14–15. A contrasting moving line begins in m. 3 and alternates throughout with the first element. If orchestrated, these could be assigned to percussive and stringed instruments as well. Envisioning an orchestration such as this may lead students to a more vibrant interpretation of this lively piece.

Minuet in D minor, BWV Appendix 132

The supple, sinuous right-hand melody blends perfectly with the angular left-hand lines, which often move in contrary motion to the melody. The B section with its broad leaps of a tenth, signaling a character change from seriousness to optimism and light, should be executed with a generous, well-balanced sound.

Musette from English Suite No. 3 in G minor, BWV 808

With its confined range and use of the tonic pedal point, this musette comes as a contrast to the more extroverted gavotte (found on p. 44) of the third English Suite. A contained sound quality with minimal dynamic inflection is suitable here as a means to evoke the rather nasal sound of the French *musette*, a small bagpipe. When performing both the gavotte and musette uninterruptedly and repeating the gavotte as indicated, the use of the una corda pedal throughout the entire musette will produce a particularly striking contrast between the two related dances, suggestive of the implied change of instrumentation.

Bourrée from Lute Suite No. 1 in E minor, BWV 996

Since the thematic material of this bourrée is quite uniform and its range rather confined (explainable by the fact that the piece was written initially for lute), one has to rely heavily on rhythmic energy and harmonic changes to generate interest and musical excitement. Avoidance of long legato lines in both hands is essential for evoking the energetic rhythmic motive of the bourrée. The second half of the piece is mainly sequential. The player is encouraged to experiment with imaginative dynamic shades and to significantly alter them in the repeat.

Musette in D Major, BWV Appendix 126

The duple meter and the absence of ornamentation in this piece suggest a quick tempo. One can imagine the left-hand part played by the *musette*, a small French bagpipe, resulting in the so-called "drone" effect. A staccato articulation on most eighth notes in the piece will convey the "drone" and somewhat nasal quality that would result if the piece were played by a combination of period wind instruments and a tambourin.

Minuet in C minor, BWV Appendix 121

Beautiful ascending lines and an abundance of chromaticism make this minuet one of the more interesting and original of the entire group. It is possible to divide the opening ascending phrase into antecedent sub-phrases, which can be articulated with a slight emphasis on the second beat.

mm. 1–4

Similarly, it is possible to group mm. 17–22 into three two-measure phrases, each one departing from a slightly higher dynamic level. The final phrase (mm. 23–24) effectively releases the tension built up by the chromaticism of the three previous phrases.

mm. 17–24

Gavotte en Rondeau from Overture in G minor, BWV 822

The *couplets* of this piece follow a harmonic plan dependent on a relationship of ascending thirds, moving from G minor to B-flat major in the first *couplet*, and subsequently to D minor in the second. A brief mode exchange on the downbeat of m. 32 establishes the main dominant, leading to the last restatement of the refrain. The rhythmic drive of this gavotte will be enhanced by the use of the suggested two-note slurs in mm. 2–3 and similar phrases, and frequent staccato and non-legato articulations in the left hand. Stressing the quarter notes and detaching the syncopated eighth notes in the middle voice in mm. 10–11, 24–25, and 28–29 will add energy to the rhythm and help distinguish the two narrow-ranged voices. Two distinct dynamic shades for each *couplet* are desirable in order to clarify the *rondeau* structure and accentuate the color of each key: lighter and softer in the first one (mm. 9–16) and somewhat fuller and broader in the second (second half of m. 24–32.)

March in E-flat Major, BWV Appendix 127

The elaborate rhythmic activity of this festive march along with the frequent use of double notes suggests a moderately fast tempo. Care should be taken to space the triplets equally within each beat, avoiding the temptation of turning them into two sixteenth-note figures followed by an eighth note. Playing the upbeats leading to mm. 2, 3, 12, 14, and 20 will add grace and enhance the expressiveness of the ensuing suspensions. The upbeats leading to mm. 9, 13, 17, and 21 require enough sound and rhythmic drive to propel each new phrase, while remaining in dynamic proportion with the preceding note.

Polonaise in G minor, BWV Appendix 125

The two opening unison phrases and the double notes in the ensuing measures suggest an imposing piece full of regal grandeur. The excerpt below suggests possible articulations.

mm. 1–4

In the repeat of the initial motive (mm. 9–10), the opposing motion of the leaps between the third beat and the preceding eighth note are a splendid surprise worth highlighting with a strong expressive accent on the third beat.

mm. 9–10

An inventive approach to the left-hand articulation will add life and interest to the sequential character of mm. 17–19.

Gavotte II from English Suite No. 6 in D minor, BWV 811

This gavotte is essentially a musette with its typical drone bass effect, resulting from the D pedal point in the left hand. The high range and close proximity of the hands require carefully balanced voicing, slightly bringing out the tenor voice without overpowering the main melody. To this end, I find the use of syncopated pedal particularly suited here. Used judiciously, it will infuse the piece with continuity and breath, and remedy the brittle sound quality sometimes peculiar to this range on the piano.

Polonaise in G Major, BWV Appendix 130

Four different elements, exposed in the successive four two-measure phrases of the first section, form the basis of this solemn, ceremonial polonaise. Ascending and descending motion alternates in these phrases, providing the performer with an opportunity for dynamic changes. Distinctly delineating the bass line of the second section will shed light on the interesting harmonic events, especially in mm. 9–10 and mm. 17–20. Applying a clear-cut dynamic contrast between the phrases in mm. 17–20 and mm. 21–22 will enhance the sudden shift of mood and the renewal of rhythmic vitality that propels the piece to its conclusion. I can clearly picture the orchestration of this piece, calling for a combination of string and wind instruments with trumpets carrying the initial phrase

Gavotte I from English Suite No. 3 in G minor, BWV 808

The broad range of this energetic and somewhat flamboyant gavotte highlights the counterpoint between melody and bass. The articulation in the left hand can alternate between staccato in the opening statement and non-legato in the middle section to differentiate the character. The sequences in mm. 10–14 will gain in interest and vitality by applying subtle phrasings, reflecting the harmonic shifts that result from the use of secondary dominants.

Minuet from Overture in F Major, BWV 820

The syncopated feel of this graceful minuet will be intensified by lightly emphasizing the dotted quarter notes in mm. 2, 5, 9, 15, and 18, and underlining the tenor voice in the first three phrases. The strong ii–V–i cadence in mm. 12–13 can be outlined by the use of non-legato articulation. A stress on the suspensions, occurring on the third beat of the tenor voice in mm. 2 and 5, followed by a softening of the resolution, is required in order to reveal their harmonic function.

Polonaise in G minor, BWV Appendix 123

The bold character of the initial right-hand statement features the typical polonaise rhythmic motive. It returns in the left hand in mm. 9–10 and may be enhanced by using a staccato–legato articulation.

mm. 1–2

In contrast, the same rhythmic figure in mm. 3 and 7 sounds more natural played legato.

mm. 3

The fingering provided in mm. 16–17 ensure a very smooth legato between the two voices in the right hand. For the left-hand line in mm. 15–17, the articulation shown below will provide a great deal of rhythmic interest and stability, suggestive of a stringed instrument such as a viola da gamba.

mm. 15–17

Gavotte from French Suite No. 5 in G Major, BWV 816

This sparkling gavotte is replete with contrary motion between the upper voices and the bass. Bringing out the polarity of the outer layers of the texture by voicing all double notes and chords will illuminate the contrapuntal ingenuity of the piece. The sudden thematic exchange between the two hands in the key of the secondary dominant in mm. 12–14 indicates a different dynamic and a shift toward a more serious character. The tempo should remain unaffected in spite of the tremendous buildup of rhythmic energy in the ending phrases (mm. 16–24.)

Minuet from French Suite No. 6 in E Major, BWV 817

The two-note slurs in this minuet and the notated appoggiaturas in m. 8 suggest an expressive accent on the first of the two quarter notes followed by a delicate release on the second. Both of these elements evoke the gentle leaping gestures of the minuet style. Adopting a moderate tempo will allow the charming melody to flourish while maintaining the dance character of this piece. The left-hand motives will gain in rhythmic interest by releasing before the leap by octave.

Scherzo from Partita No. 3 in A minor, BWV 827

The continuous flow of sixteenth notes in 2/4, combined with the presence of little ornamentation and the uncomplicated harmonic rhythm, suggests a rather brisk tempo. The two distinct motives of this boisterous piece can be characterized by using various degrees of articulation in the left hand: sturdier, heavier accented chords in the first (mm. 1–4) and softer, more scintillating staccato eighth notes in the second (mm. 4–9). The sinuous contours of the sub-phrases will come to life by employing clear dynamics and sensible phrasing as suggested.

Sarabande from English Suite No. 5 in E minor, BWV 810

The first section of this magnificent sarabande lends itself to a long dynamic arc through its continuously ascending phrases. The quietly sorrowful melodic motive of the opening phrase progressively rises with inner tranquility and dignity, reaching its peak point in m. 7. The second section, beginning in m. 9, reflects the spirit of quiet contemplation and tenderness, with internal voices interacting in contrary motion. Properly applied, the designated staccatos over the eighth notes in m. 1 and in analogous melodic gestures (such as in mm. 7, 15, and 23) will give a more uplifting, yet dignified allure to the music and prevent the feeling of sternness that might result from an overly heavy, grounded approach.

Minuet I from French Suite No. 2 in C minor, BWV 813

The original manuscript of this minuet, unlike most of the other dances, contains a number of articulation markings. The presence of two types of slurs, one starting on the second of a six eighth-note figure (m. 1), and the other on the first (m. 13), implies a different manner of performance respectively: in the first case the first eighth note should be slightly detached, while in the second all the notes should sound legato.

mm. 1 and 13

Other articulation signs present in the original manuscript include the two-note slurs in mm. 3–4 and the staccatos in the IV–V–I cadence of m. 7. To my mind, the presence of these elements in the original demonstrate that the use of varied articulation is intended in all minuets and that cadencial points are better emphasized by a detached articulation. Adhering to these valuable indications will naturally prevent the student from adopting too slow a pace or too heavy a touch.

Prelude from Suite in F minor, BWV 823

Considering the thirty-second notes in mm. 41–49 and elsewhere, caution should be exercised not to start this piece at too fast a tempo. The overall form, a *rondeau*, consists of an eight-bar principal theme restated four times with varied *couplets* in between. The unchanged descending stepwise harmonic progression of the variations is typical of seventeenth- and eighteenth-century variation forms, such as the *chaconne* or *passacaglia*. Clear delineation of the texture and strong characterization of each variation by means of articulation and dynamics will shed light as to the rhythmic and melodic contours of this grandiose musical edifice.

—*Christos Tsitsaros*

References

Bach, Carl Philipp Emanuel. *Essay on the True Art of Playing Keyboard Instruments*. Edited and translated by William J. Mitchel. New York: W. W. Norton & Company, Inc., 1949.

Ferguson, Howard. *Keyboard Interpretation from the 14th to the 19th Century*. New York and London: Oxford University Press, 1975.

Geiringer, Karl. *Johann Sebastian Bach. The Culmination of an Era*. New York: Oxford University Press, 1966.

Source for the music contained in this edition: Bach, Johann Sebastian. *Neue Ausgabe Sämtlicher Werke (Neue Bach Ausgabe)*, ed. Johann-Sebastian-Bach-Institut. Göttligen, and Bach-Archiv, Leipzig. Kassel and Basle, 1954.

A special note of thanks to Mr. Chris Pawlicki, technical assistant of the music library at the University of Illinois, Urbana-Champaign, for his invaluable help in locating the original sources for the music.

Minuet in G Major

Christian Petzold
BWV Appendix 114

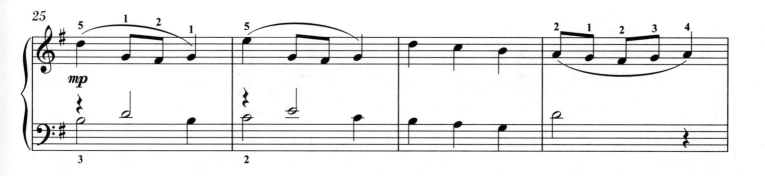

Minuet in G minor

Christian Petzold
BWV Appendix 115

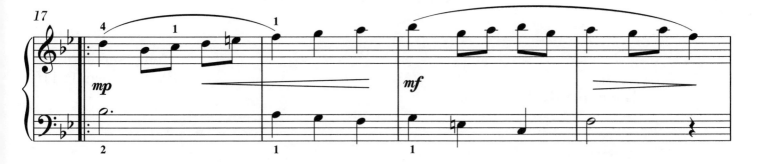

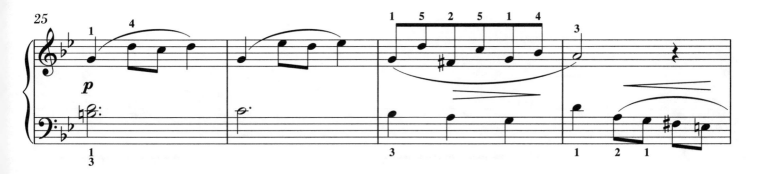

Minuet in G Major

Composer unknown
BWV Appendix 116

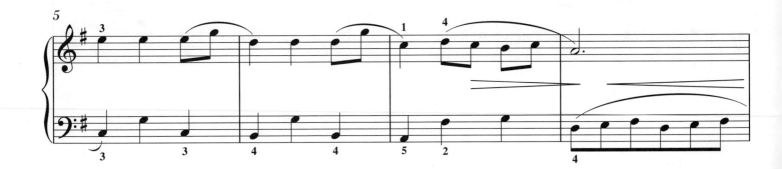

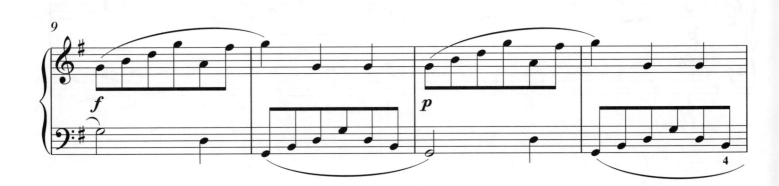

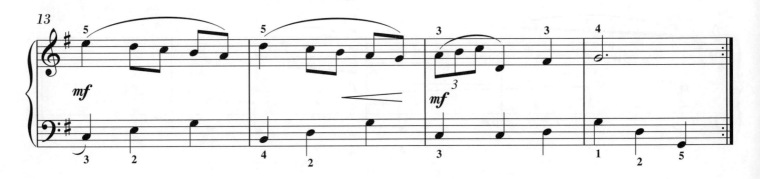

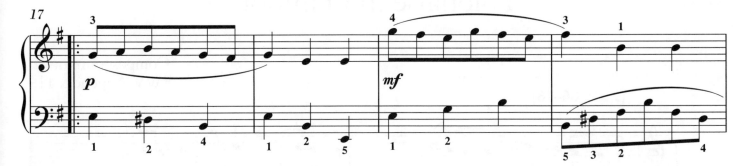

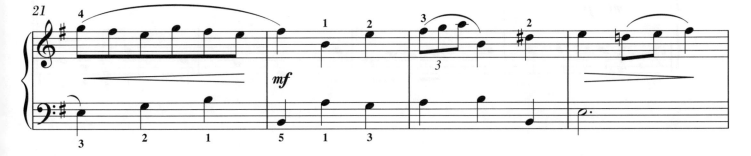

Polonaise in G minor

Composer unknown
BWV Appendix 119

*These wedge markings appear in the source manuscript.

Minuet 1
from Overture in G minor

Johann Sebastian Bach
BWV 822

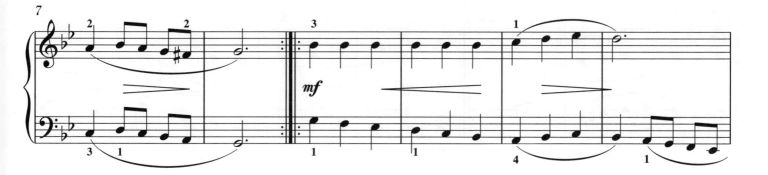

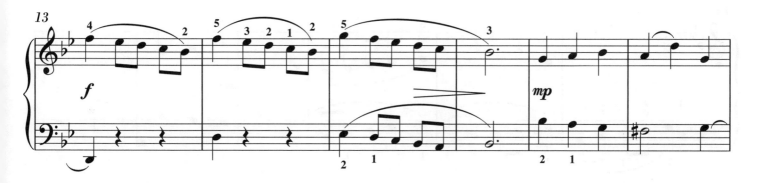

May perform all three Minuets from Overture in G minor as a group in the following order: 1–2–1–3–1.

Minuet 2
from Overture in G minor

Johann Sebastian Bach
BWV 822

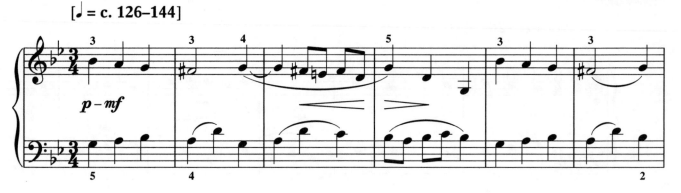

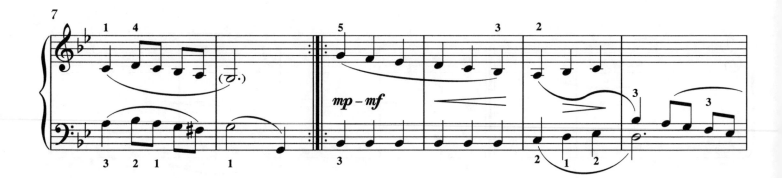

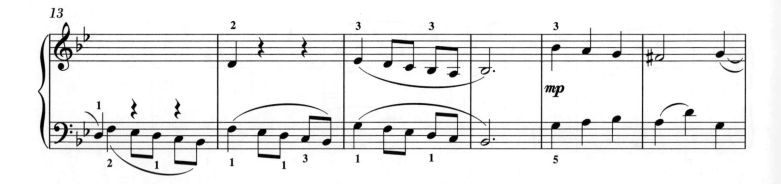

Minuet 1 is on page 19.

(Minuet 1 da capo)

Minuet 3
from Overture in G minor

Johann Sebastian Bach
BWV 822

[♩ = c. 126–144]

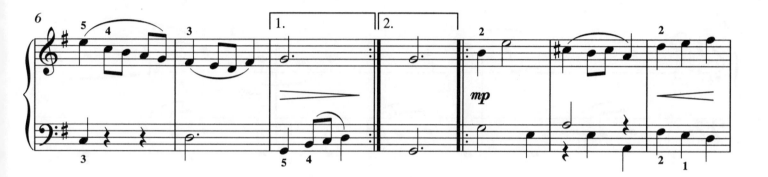

Minuet 1 is on page 19.

(Minuet 1 da capo)

March in D Major

C.P.E. Bach
BWV Appendix 122

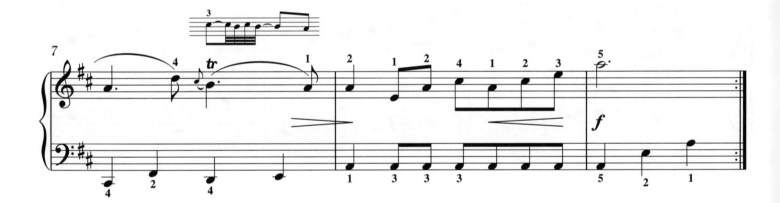

March in G Major

C.P.E. Bach
BWV Appendix 124

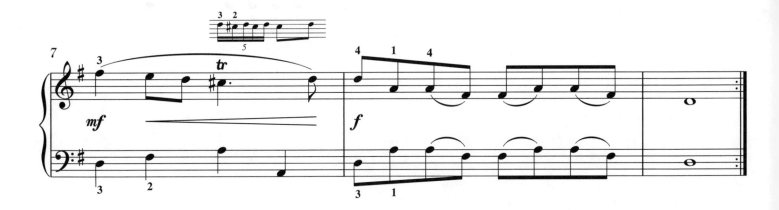

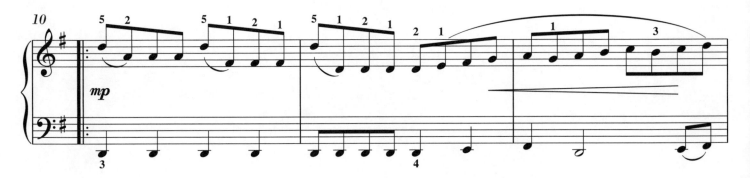

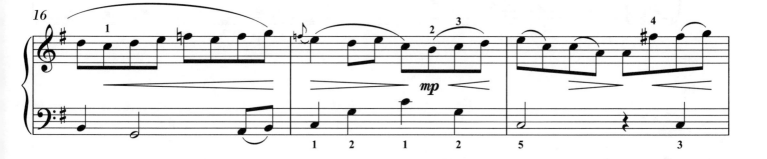

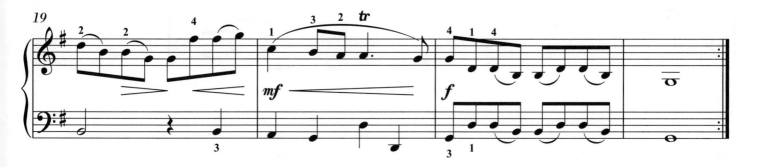

Minuet in D minor

Composer unknown
BWV Appendix 132

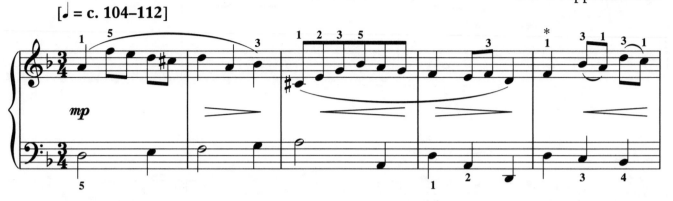

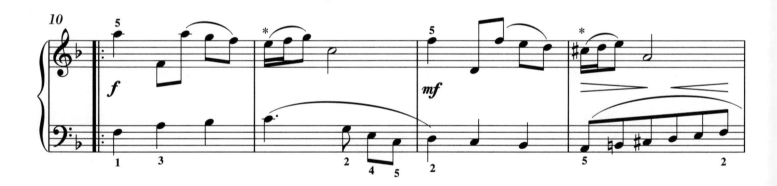

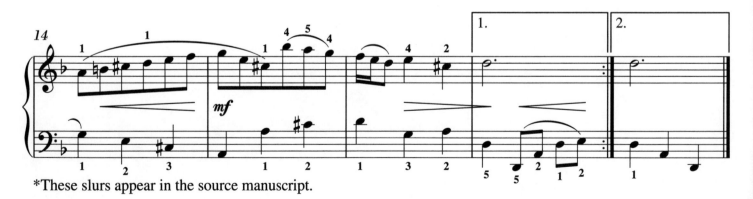

*These slurs appear in the source manuscript.

Musette
from English Suite No. 3 in G minor

Johann Sebastian Bach
BWV 808

* These two-note slurs appear in the source manuscript.

** This piece can be performed with Gavotte I on p. 44 as a set in this order: Gavotte I–Musette–Gavotte I.
   See Performance Notes for Musette.

(Repeat Gavotte I)

Bourrée
from Lute Suite No. 1 in E minor

Johann Sebastian Bach
BWV 996

[♩ = c. 76–84]

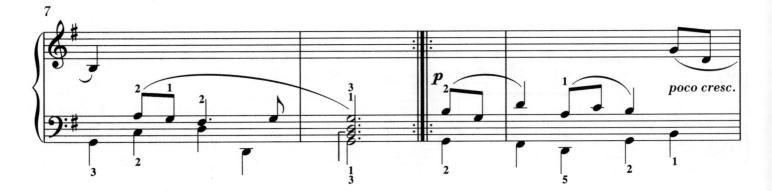

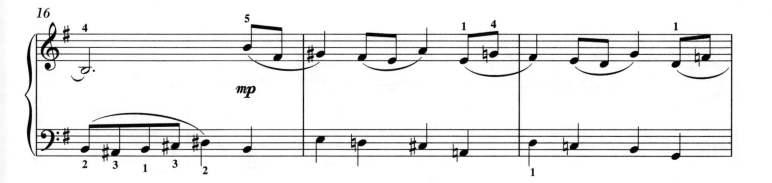

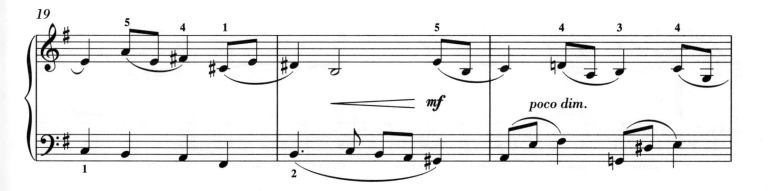

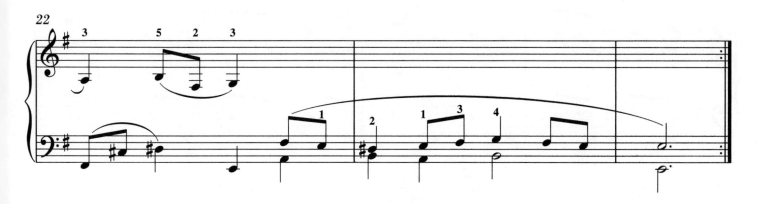

Musette in D Major

Composer unknown
BWV Appendix 126

[♩ = c. 69–80]

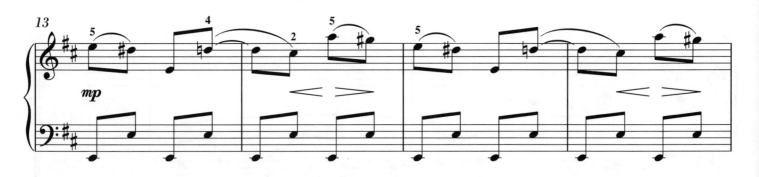

Minuet in C minor

Composer unknown
BWV Appendix 121

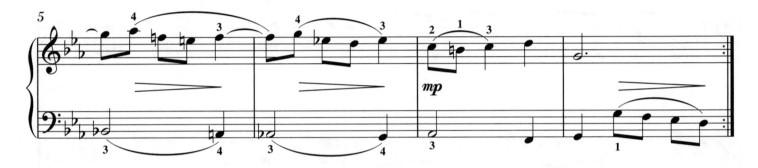

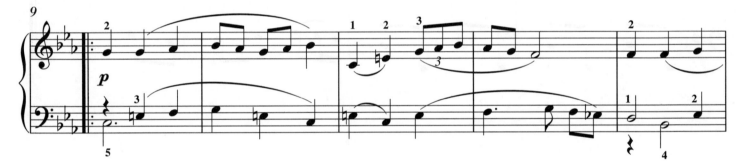

Minuet
from Overture in F Major

Johann Sebastian Bach
BWV 820

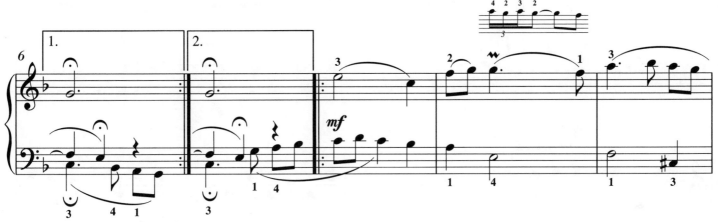

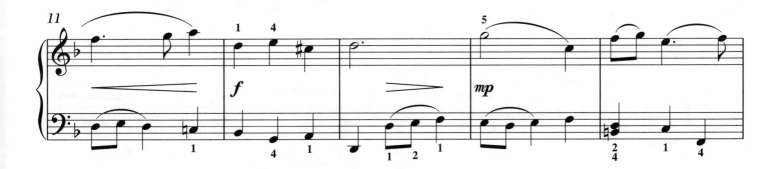

*Play small notes second time.

Gavotte en Rondeau
from Overture in G minor

Johann Sebastian Bach
BWV 822

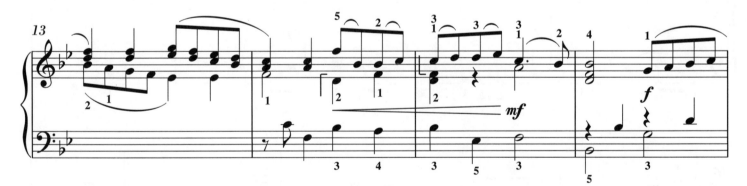

March in E-flat Major

Johann Sebastian Bach
BWV Appendix 127

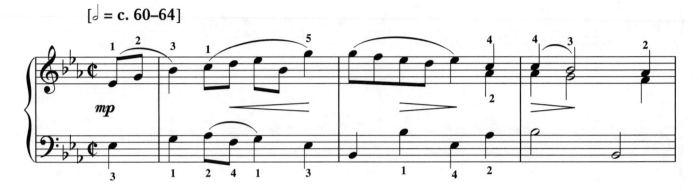

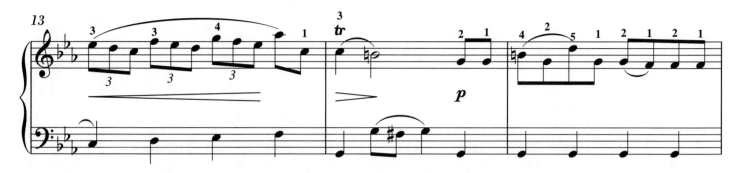

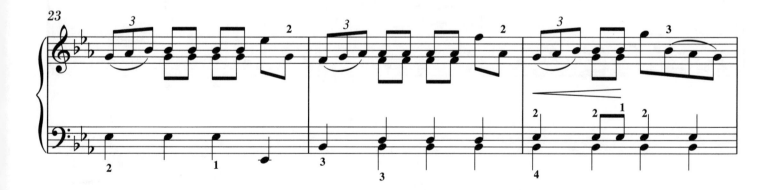

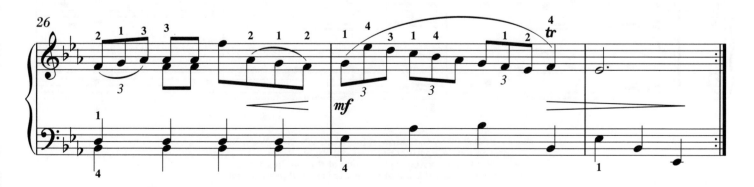

Polonaise in G minor

C.P.E. Bach
BWV Appendix 125

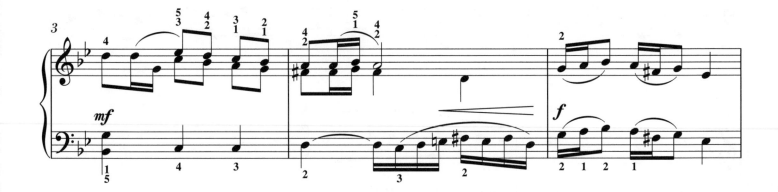

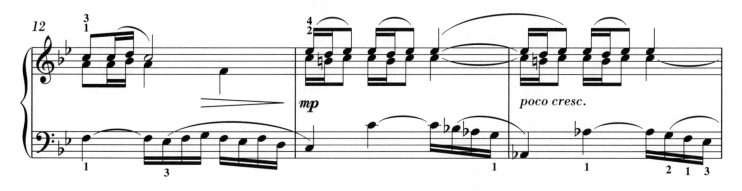

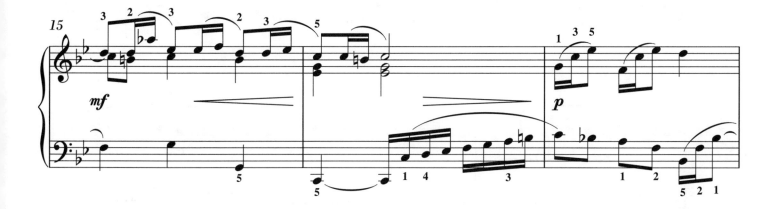

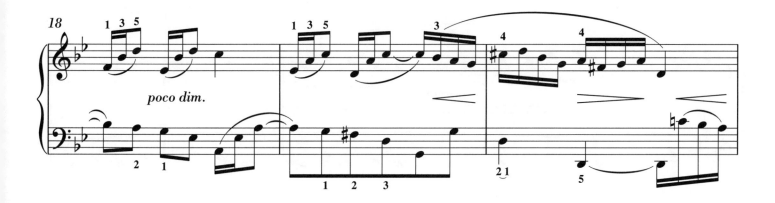

Gavotte II
from English Suite No. 6 in D minor

Johann Sebastian Bach
BWV 811

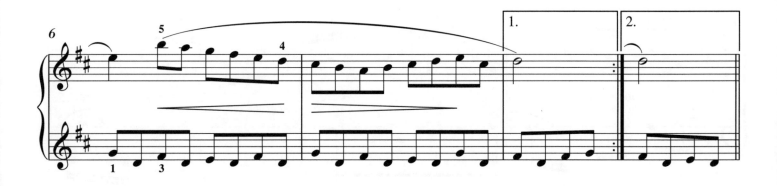

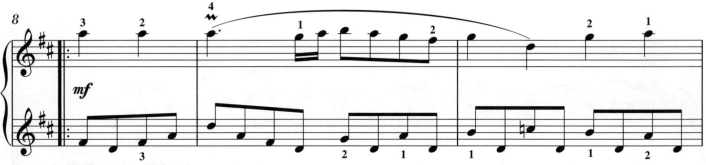

* Alternate fingering is for the repeat.

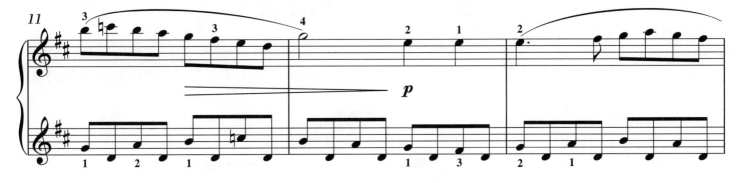

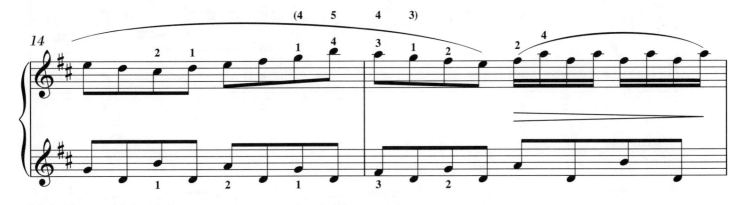

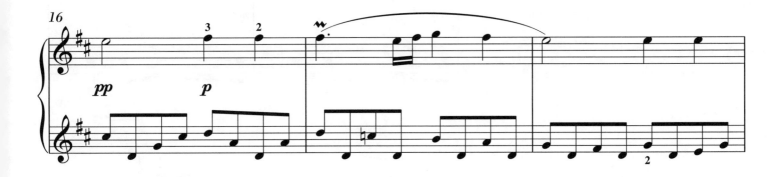

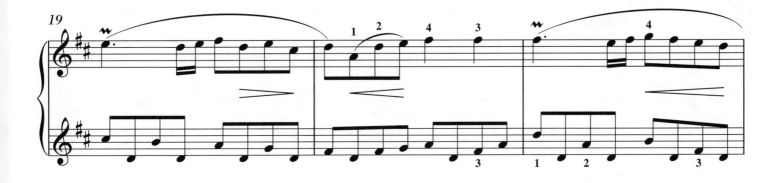

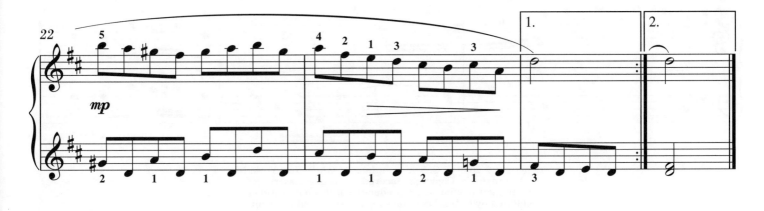

Polonaise in G Major

Johann Sebastian Bach
BWV Appendix 130

[♩ = c. 72–80]

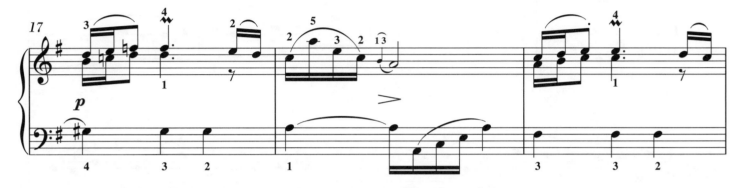

Gavotte I
from English Suite No. 3 in G minor

Johann Sebastian Bach
BWV 808

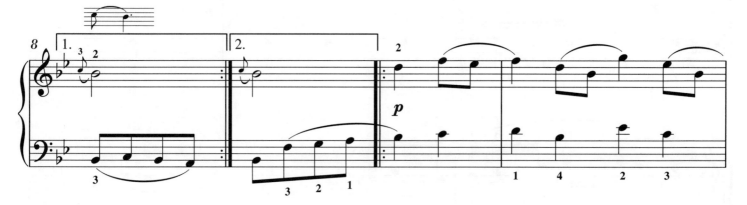

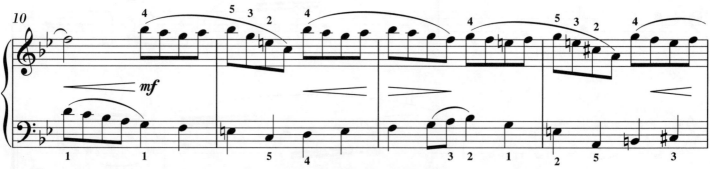

* These slur markings are in the source manuscript; all other indications are editorial.

** This piece can be performed with the Musette on p. 27 as a set in this order: Gavotte I–Musette–Gavotte I.

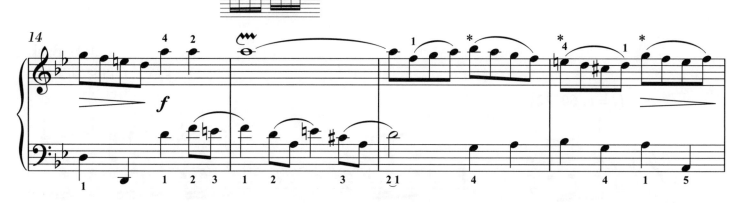

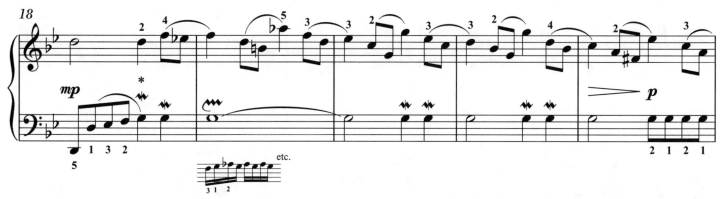

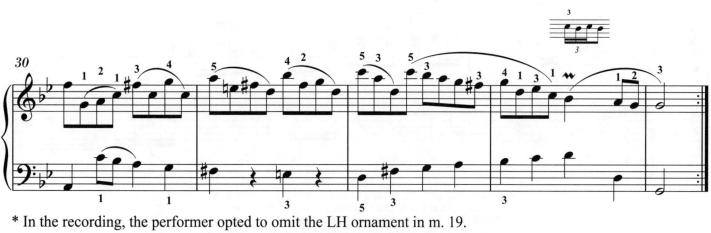

* In the recording, the performer opted to omit the LH ornament in m. 19.

Polonaise in G minor

C.P.E. Bach
BWV Appendix 123

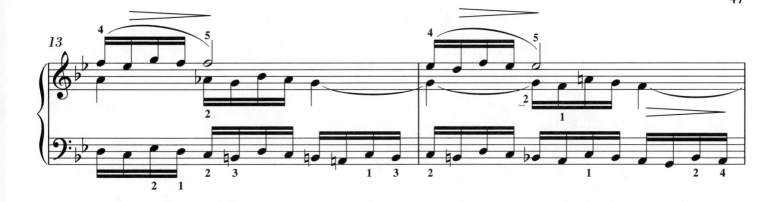

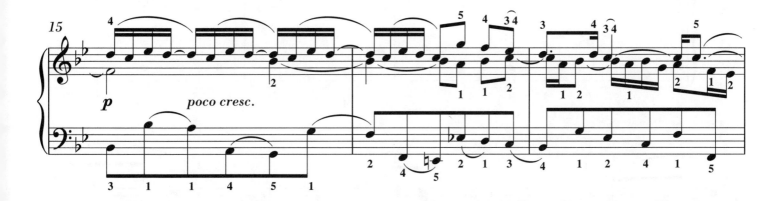

Gavotte
from French Suite No. 5 in G Major

Johann Sebastian Bach
BWV 816

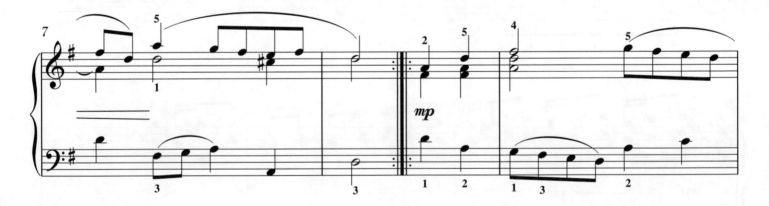

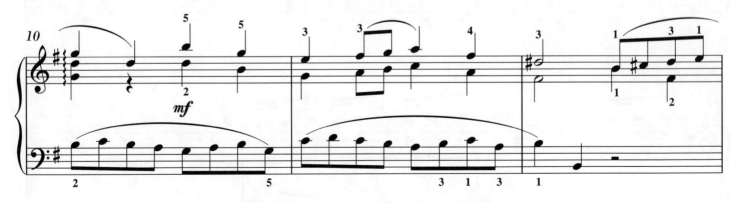

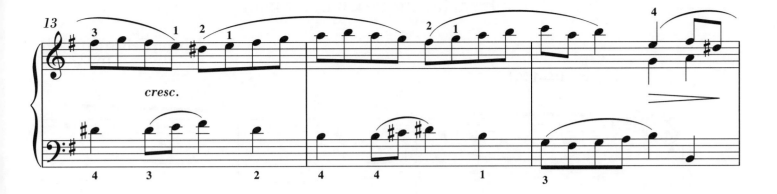

Minuet
from French Suite No. 6 in E Major

Johann Sebastian Bach
BWV 817

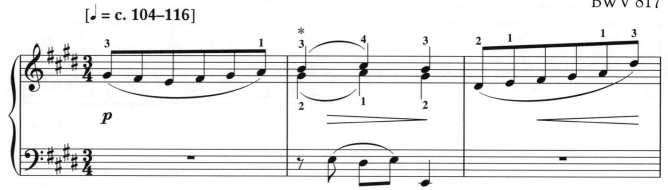

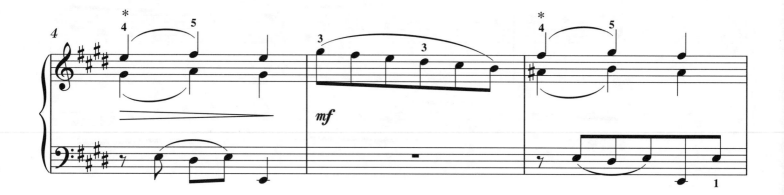

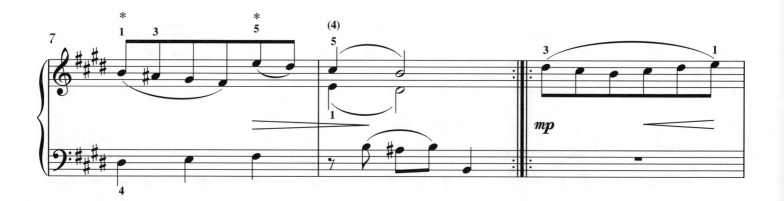

* These slur markings appear in the source manuscript.

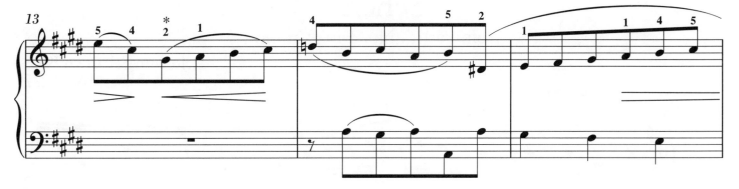

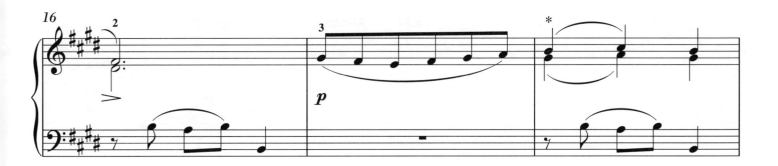

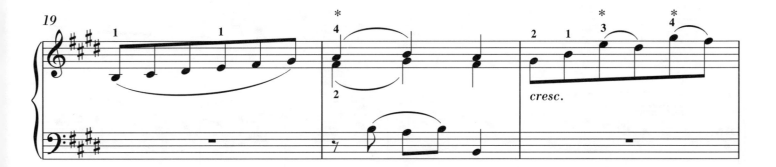

Scherzo
from Partita No. 3 in A minor

Johann Sebastian Bach
BWV 827

[♩ = c. 84–94]

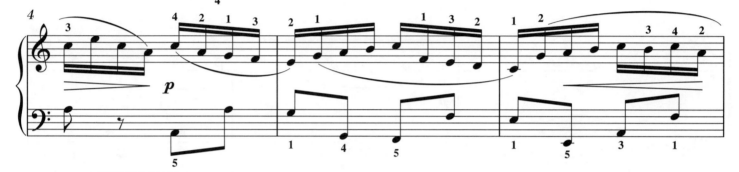

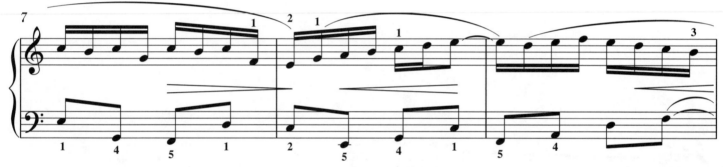

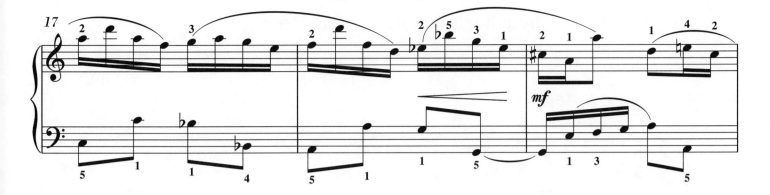

Sarabande
from English Suite No. 5 in E minor

Johann Sebastian Bach
BWV 810

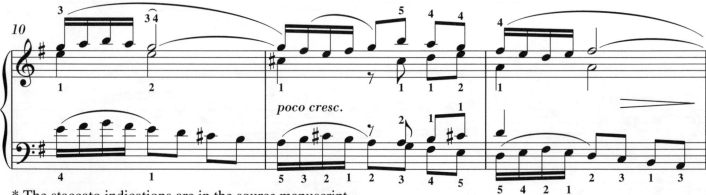

* The staccato indications are in the source manuscript.

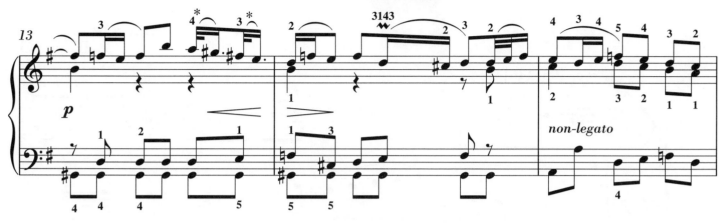

* These two slurs are indicated in the source manuscript.

Minuet I
from French Suite No. 2 in C minor

Johann Sebastian Bach
BWV 813

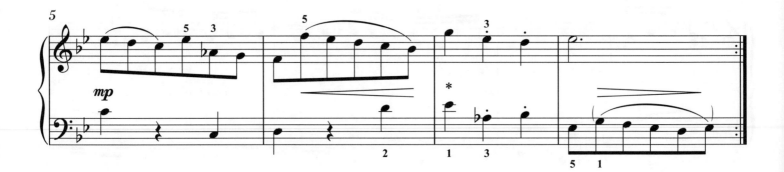

* All slurs appear in the source manuscript, except those in parenthesis, as do the staccatos in m. 7.

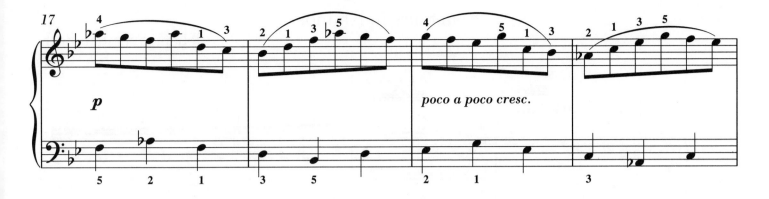

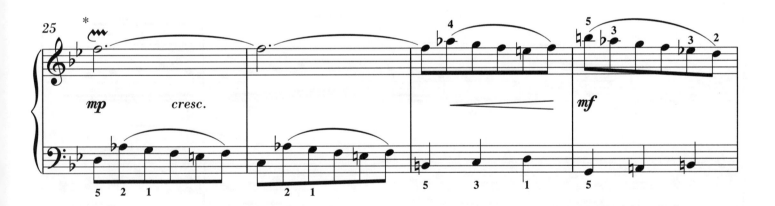

Prelude
from Suite in F minor

Johann Sebastian Bach
BWV 823

* These slur indications are found in the source manuscript.

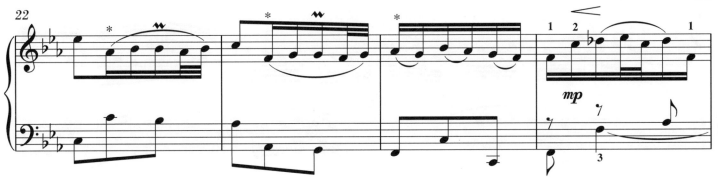

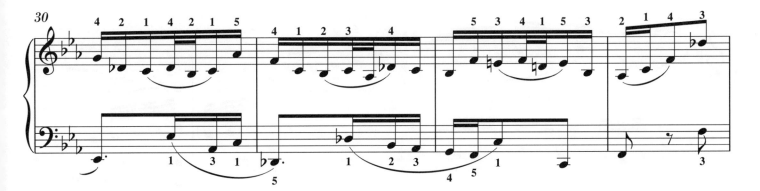

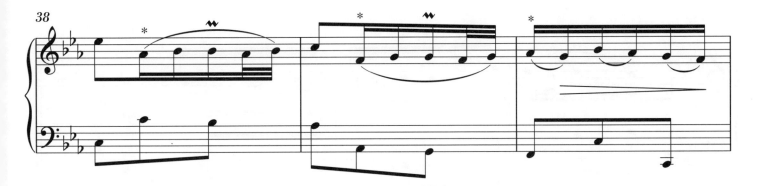

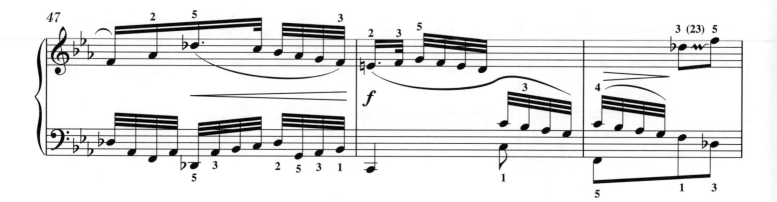

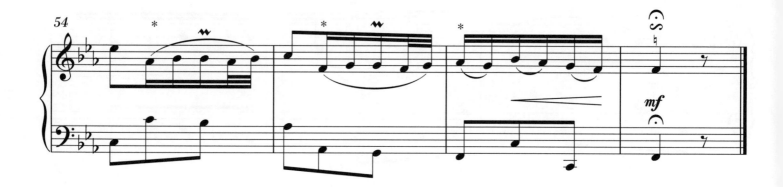

ABOUT THE EDITOR

Christos Tsitsaros

Christos Tsitsaros, contributing composer and arranger for the Hal Leonard Student Piano Library, is Associate Professor of Piano Pedagogy at the University of Illinois. Born in Nicosia, Cyprus, he received his first formal instruction at the Greek Academy of Music. At the age of thirteen, he won first prize at the National Competition of the Conservatory of Athens. He later continued his musical studies at the Chopin Academy of Warsaw and later in Paris, receiving the Diplôme Supérieur d'Exécution with distinction. In 1986, a scholarship from the A. G. Leventis Foundation enabled him to pursue further development at the School of Music of Indiana University, where he received an Artist Diploma and a Masters degree (1989). He attained a Doctor of Musical Arts in Piano Performance from the University of Illinois (1993). His mentors include pianists Jan Ekier, Aldo Ciccolini, Jean-Claude Pennetier, Germaine Mounier, Gÿorgy Sebök, and Ian Hobson.

Dr. Tsitsaros has participated in various workshops and conferences as a performer and lecturer, and has appeared as soloist and recitalist in Europe, the United States, and Canada. In 2001, he gave his New York debut recital at Weill Carnegie Hall. Two CD recordings of his original piano compositions are available on the Centaur label. He currently serves as Piano Chair for the Illinois State Music Teachers Association.